William Bennett

The first baby in camp.

A full account of the scenes and adventures during the pioneer days of

'49. George Francis Train.-Staging in early days.-A mad, wild ride.-The

pony express.-Some of the old time drivers

William Bennett

The first baby in camp.
A full account of the scenes and adventures during the pioneer days of '49. George Francis Train.-Staging in early days.-A mad, wild ride.-The pony express.-Some of the old time drivers

ISBN/EAN: 9783337727680

Printed in Europe, USA, Canada, Australia, Japan

Cover: Foto ©ninafisch / pixelio.de

More available books at **www.hansebooks.com**

...THE...

FIRST BABY IN CAMP.

A FULL ACCOUNT OF THE SCENES AND AD-
VENTURES DURING THE PIONEER
DAYS OF '49.

GEORGE FRANCIS TRAIN.—STAGING IN EARLY DAYS.—
A MAD, WILD RIDE.—THE PONY EXPRESS.—
SOME OF THE OLD TIME DRIVERS.

By WM. P. BENNETT, Author of "The Sky-Sifter."

The fastest time made in Nevada by Stage, Pony Express or Buckboard, 22 miles in 58 minutes.

(Picture 22x28 accompanies this book.)

THE RANCHER PUBLISHING CO.,

Salt Lake City, Utah.

1893.

INDEX.

two or three days and asked to be shown the nugget, some arriving from camps eight or ten miles distant.

The baby brought luck with it, for on the day it was born Wilson made a big find in his claim. He struck a crevice that was piled full of coarse gold. He took out $3,000 in one pan. It was all in nuggets, the largest of which was worth over $300.

The only other woman on Canyon Creek at the time of the first baby episode was Mrs. Bill Tibbits, a sister of Mrs. Wilson. Bill Wilson was a Mormon and went back to Salt Lake so well stocked with gold that he was able to afford the luxury of three wives.

It is not probable, however, that any child born to him in Mormondom caused a tenth part of the excitement incident to the birth of his first in the cabin on Canyon Creek. Even after the joke about the "nugget" became known many men dropped in to see the child on its own merits. The miners were proud to be able to say they had a baby in camp.

The boys on Canyon Creek caused to be made for Mrs. Wilson a ring, which was a circle of small specimens o polished gold quartz linked together with pure gold of their own digging.

FIRST BABY IN CAMP.

In the good old days when '49ers
   Thought of little else than gold,
'Twas then a woman in the camp
   They rarely did behold.
It must not be surprising if,
   Indulging in a tramp,
They did gaze with joy and wonder
   At the first babe in the camp.

Here you see an honest fellow,
  Excitement in his eyes,
Gazing on the little darling
  As it for mama cries;
Its little arms uplifted tells
  Its wants in plantive notes,
While the mother, with smiling face,
  Upon her loved one dotes.

'Tis a scene of joy and pleasure,
  A reminder of the past,
To those honest, rustic fellows
  Who, from home and dear ones cast,
Found a refuge where blessed nature
  Had kept for them in store
Many a glorious fortune
  In the good old days of yore.

The baby in the camp to them
  Was a source of much delight,
It made them think of dear old home
  Ere from it they took their flight.
In many a heart still lingers
  Impressions of that tramp,
When the good old honest miner
  Saw the first babe in camp.

GEORGE FRANCIS TRAIN.

A WILD EXPERIENCE—THE WILDEST OF HIS LIFE.

George Francis Train, whose name and fame have been spread over two continents and whose strange eccentricity has made him a character sought after in all sections of our country, as a lecturer, could draw the biggest house of any man upon the boards and as a sensationalist he had no equal.

Train had received an invitation to lecture in Virginia City and on his way there he had to encounter the usual episode connected with stage driving over the Sierra Nevada mountains, but his experience was not so extended as was Horace Greeley's for Train had to travel from Reno to Virginia City, only, as the railroad was completed to Reno and the cars were running to that point.

August 24, 1869, on the arrival of the cars at Reno, W. P. Bennett, with a Wells, Fargo & Co. racing buckboard with two horses, and the Pacific Express Co. (Pony) with rider mounted in the saddle, were just about starting on one of their liveliest races for Virginia City when the famous George Francis Train, who had just arrived, rushed up to Bennett saying:

"You're Mr. Bennett, and you're going to Virginia City, are you not?"

"Yes, sir! right now. Talk quick for I must be off directly."

"My name is George Francis Train. I am to lecture at Virginia City to-night, and Mr. Latham telegraphed me that I could ride up with you, if you thought—"

"But I can't. Damn if I'm going to let that pony beat me on account of George Francis Train or anybody else."

"But I'm billed to—"

"All right! Jump aboard, quick! Let 'em go!"

And with a slap, dash and fierce jerk as the express bag was tossed onto the buckboard, away they went amid cheering yells from the excited crowd of spectators. There was nearly as much excitement at the start as there was at the finish, for it was a hot contest for superiority and every minute's delay seemed like a week to the drivers. Over the bridge across the Truchee they bounced out onto the Virginia road, George Francis holding fast to his seat and his breath at the same time.

> There was no time to think or joke
> On such a trip as that.
> Train, do not let your hold get broke
> And watch out for your hat.

As they flew down the first slope or declevity south of the bridge, Train's hat danced off, notwithstanding the warning already given him and Bennett impatiently drew up a moment and George recovered his hat.

"That's all right this time," says Bennett, "but next time your hat stays behind."

Poor Train was to be pitied; the flying gravel and sharp dodging seemed to be more than he could bear. Bennett wore a veil extending from the rim of his hat down over his face to protect it from the sharp pebbles and gravel spitefully thrown back from the heels of the flying mustangs while George Francis dodged and was blinded by the severe infliction until Bennett compasionately tore off a p ece of his face-protector and gave it to him.

> He pitied the sorrows of poor old Train
> But he had to get there on time
> And of all the tricks considered vain
> To get in first was mine.   .

Near Huffaker's Station, a small bridge over a muddy

little creek was obstructed by a ten-mule team which was
coming. Bennett promptly dodged the bridge and jumped
the stream, the mud and water from heels and wheels
spattering them finely.

"Don't let go of anything. Hang on and don't be afraid,"
said Bennett.

George Francis' eager attention to the general outlook
was too fully occupied for any reply.

LIGHTNING CHANGES.

Six changes of horses were made on the trip, about
twenty-two miles, each change occupying merely a few seconds, the fresh horses standing ready harnessed, with plenty
of active men with quick hands attending to the matter, a
man to each strap or buckle. In fact the buckboard would
merely have come to a stand still before Bennett, grabbing
the lines thrown to him, sang out, "let 'em go," and away
they did go like a comet with a long dusty tail streaming
out behind.

The somewhat slower rush up the steep Geiger grade
gave George a chance to collect his bewildered ideas, and
his wind, and regain his speech. Never, in the world, had
he ever experienced such

A MAD, WILD RIDE.

He felt nervously paralyzed and held onto his seat like grim
death, especially after passing the Six Mile House and the
Summit of the Grade. He owned up that he was somewhat inclined to be frightened about that time for now they
went tearing and plunging more furiously than ever along
the level and downward grades approaching Virginia
City.

Near the Sierra Nevada Mining Works, another one of
those obstacles, in the form of a big hay team heavily laden,
stood in the middle of the road, blockading the way completely, and Bennett, knowing no such word as fail, at once
plunged his firey team over the grade, down through sage
brush and rocks and around up onto the road again, right
side up and nobody hurt.   Train's hair fairly stood on end.
He set his teeth together, his eyes glared and his tongue
was paralyzed.

> This was indeed an episode
> That would fore'er his memory load,
> And Bennett's name would linger till
> Death had made him cold and still.

A GRAND RECEPTION MISCONSTRUED BY TRAIN.

The flying buckboard was not long in dashing in on "C"
Street, which was the principle street of the town.   The
sidewalks were densely crowded, the tops of the houses and
the balconies ditto—the masses of humanity watching the
race and yelling to their heart's content.   Hats were thrown
in the air and handkerchiefs waved on every side.   George
Francis felt much relieved and very glorious; he evidently
considered that this was a grand, spontaneous, popular ova-
tion to himself, personally, and most graciously and grace-
fully did he bow and lift his hat to the admiring multitude
on every side; all that he could see lacking was a brass band
playing "Hail to the Chief."   With a sudden serge, they
came to a sudden stand-still in front of Wells, Fargo & Co.'s
office.   When those wild mustangs were brought to a quick
stand-still, they reared up on their hind legs and seemed to
be disappointed at being brought to so sudden a halt.

The race was over.   Distance, 22 miles; time, one hour
and ten minutes.

When they had alighted from the buckboard, George could not help wondering why nobody seemed to recognize him or rush forward to shake hands.

This scene was only a repetition of those happening every day, and the racers were watched for with so much eagerness that many of the spectators grew wildly frantic.

It was now 6 o'clock, P.M. Popular excitement subsided, Wells, Fargo winning, and when somebody said, "That was George Francis Train on there with Bennett," people remembered that he was going to lecture at the Opera House.

TRAIN'S LECTURE.

That evening George Francis Train lectured to a $215.00 audience, the house being tolerably well filled. It was a rambling, entertaining sort of an address, vigorous in style, yet not giving much in the way of solid argument or important information. Everybody seemed to enjoy it, however, and declared they got their money's worth. The most interesting part of his lecture was his reference to the ride to Virginia City from Reno. He said he had traveled in Europe, on the ocean and everywhere else, by the swiftest conveyances, and on top of and behind the fastest horses or anything else that anybody had, but that buckboard, Bennett and his wild mustangs had more chain-lightning, snap and fierce reckless dash in them than anything he had ever experienced or ever cared to again. It was the liveliest hour and ten minutes of his life.

STAGING IN EARLY DAYS.

REMINISCENCES OF PERILOUS TRIPS ACROSS THE SIERRA NEVADAS.

VALENTINE'S ROUGH EXPERIENCE—OLD TIME STAGE DRIVERS. —SOME FAST TRIPS—PONIES AND BUCKBOARDS.

Those were the days, the good old days,
  When "knights of the whip" stood high;
When men would cheer and ladies praise
And children in surprise would gaze
  On the heroes drawing nigh.
They were all monarchs in those times
If they could handle stage coach lines.

All old residents of Virginia City and San Francisco
know that in early days of "Washoe" and the Comstock
lode some perilous trips were made by stage coaches
across the Sierra Nevadas. On numerous occasions great
hardships were endured by both drivers and passengers.
It is not necessary to give the "rough trips" in detail, a
few samples will be sufficient.

VALENTINE'S ROUGH TRIP.

In 1867 Mr. Valentine, then agent of Wells, Fargo & Co.
at Virginia City, now Vice-president and General Manager
of the company on the Pacific coast, crossed the mountains under peculiarly ardurous circumstances. On or about

the night of February 21 a heavy snow storm set in at
Virginia and it was reported to be snowing heavily in the
main Sierra Nevadas. At 5 o'clock on the morning of the
22nd Mr. Valentine left Virginia for California by the Placerville route, on a two-horse sleigh with three companions,
including the driver. They reached VanSickle's Station,
two miles south of Genoa, at 5 o'clock P. M., having traveled
thirty-three miles. Here they halted for the night, being at
the foot of the Kingsburg grade over the main Sierra Nevada range.

HARD ROAD TO TRAVEL.

Next morning, with a small army of assistants, they started
to encounter the deeper snow and drifts of the mountain
road. By hard pushing and shoveling they managed to
get near Peterson's station, four miles, and returned to
VanSickle's for the night. Early next morning they returned to Peterson's where they left the sleigh, and Valentine, with three companions, took to Norwegian snow shoes.
By 2 o'clock P. M. they had crossed the eastern summit of
the Sierra Nevadas, and at 7:30 in the evening they passed
Friday's station, arriving at Billy Mack's place about 11
o'clock, fourteen miles from VanSickle's. It is unnecessary
to remark that Valentine, as well as his companions,
did some very good sleeping that night. Next morning
they resumed their hard journey over the wild waste of
snow from fifteen to twenty feet in depth. Owing to the
lightness of the freshly fallen snow, it was found to be very
difficult traveling, as the long snow shoes would sink several inches into the feathery mass instead of skimming
along on the surface as on the snow that has settled and
become compact. At noon they stopped for an hour at
Yank's station, at the head of Lake Tahoe, for rest, and re-

freshment, having made six miles, one mile an hour, since
6 o'clock, when they left Billy Mack's.

They passed over the western summit of the Sierras
about 5:30 P. M. and arrived safely but very tired at the
hotel in Strawberry valley at 1 o'clock in the morning, having completely and appreciatively crossed the famous old
Sierra Nevadas; the last eighteen miles being accomplished in eighteen hours amid a furious storm.

The dismal nature of Valentine's trip may be imagined
when it is remembered that upon all sides lay a rugged
wilderness, with nothing to be seen even in day light but
rocks and forests and naught to be heard but the wild howl-
ing of the winds in the tops of the tall pines.

> Dismal scenes of rugged wildwood
> Extending o'er the drifted snow,
> Surprised the tourist on his journey
> As he traveled sure and slow.

The snow at this time was about seven feet deep in the
valleys, and on the mountains about level with the tops of
the telegraph poles.

On the fifth day of his trip, Valentine left Strawberry at
6 o'clock in the morning on board of a "scow," being a con-
glomerate sort of a craft suitable for navigating melting
snow, water or liquid mud. This vehicle of novel construc-
tion was propelled by six horses, driven by that famous
whip, "Curly Dan." They reached Placerville at 8 o'clock
that evening, having traveled forty-nine miles, here ending
the difficulties and dangers of Mr. Valentine's famous trip.
From there down to Folsom could only be at the worst,
rainy, muddy and disagreeable.

SOME FAST TRIPS.

Having given a sample of the rough trips without touching upon those attended by loss of life, a few specimens of fast time will not be out of place. The first fast trip across the Sierras of which everybody has heard was in 1862, from Carson City to Placerville by the Pioneer stage line, Hank Monk driver, and Horace Greely passenger. The time made between the two points was twelve hours, distance one hundred and twelve miles. Another fast trip was made in 1864, from Virginia City to Sacramento. Charley Croall drove from Virginia to Yank's, Hank Monk thence to Strawberry and Charley Watson to Placerville. Passengers left Virginia City at 12:10 P. M. and taking the rail road at Folsom, were landed in Sacramento at 11 A. M. the next day, distance 158 miles, time less than twelve hours.

In October 1865 a fast trip was made between Virginia City and Folsom, by which passengers were landed at Sacramento in twelve hours and twenty-one minutes. On this trip John Spaulding, afterwards promoted agent by Wells Fargo & Co., was driver from Virginia City to Strawberry, Wm. Taylor thence to Placerville and Jerry Cowder to Folsom. Some good time was also made between Virginia City and Carson. July, 1864, Ned Hudson and John Spaulding on the seat, carrying mail, express, baggage and six passengers, made the distance of eighteen miles in sixty-three minutes, changing horses at Mound House and express at Gold Hill and Silver City. They drove six horses and the time made was very fast, distance, load and stoppages being considered.

THE PONY EXPRESS.

All old residents of the Pacific cost will remember the

great Pony express across the plains in the early days, also the incident of a Sacramento lady placing a garland of flowers upon the first pony when he arrived in that city. Even in 1863 our latest news from the Atlantic seaboard came by pony. "Cockeyed Bob" (Haslin) and other celebrated riders of the plains are still greatfully remembered by reporters and many others on the Comstock. The swift riders gathered news as they flew, and told us the movements of Indian tribes and of the latest pranks in Mormondom, for at that time the umbilical cord had not been severed by which we were attached to Utah. It was cut March 20, 1861.

In 1868 Wells, Fargo & Co. and the Pacific Express Co. ran ponies in lively opposition between Reno and Virginia City. Each company had twenty-four horses on the route, running twelve, with four riders at each trip, distance twenty-one miles. The first race was won by Wells, Fargo & Co., time, sixty-one and sixty-five minutes, respectively. In October, 1869, they had another big race, Wells, Fargo & Co. winning. Time, fifty-eight and sixty-four minutes, respectively.

BUCKBOARD EXPRESS RIVALRY.

In 1869 light two-horse buckboard wagons were placed upon the route by Wells, Fargo & Co. for better convenience in carrying express matter, and there were some very exciting races between them and the Pacific ponies. One trip was made, W. P. Bennett driver, accompanied by the writer of this, in one hour and five minutes, beating the Pacific pony two minutes, and the time subsequently made by George Francis Train, five minutes.

INTRODUCTION.

The following pages contain some very interesting reminiscences concerning life in the early days among the mountain fastnesses and the wild plains of the far west, a history of staging in the Sierras, including fast trips and fast time of stage, pony express and buckboard, also perilous trips in snow and storm, with a sketch of Hank Monk and all the famous old-time drivers on the Placerville and Henness Pass routes, gold mining in California in the days of '49, with many incidents and adventures, both grave and gay, illustrative of the life of the miner, and a hundred other things dear to the heart of every old Pioneer.

These sketches are intended to more thoroughly explain the different scenes portrayed in the large colored engraving entitled "The Pioneers' Ten Commandments," which accompanies this book. There is also a set of 200 other engravings illustrating historical incidents extending from 1789 to 1893, which may be procured by addressing the author.

There are still for sale a few copies of "The Sky Sifter," a strange and thrilling tale of life among the Indians. Address   WM. P. BENNETT,
Salt Lake City, Utah.

THE FIRST BABY IN CAMP.

On the 25th day of December, 1849, on Canyon Creek, two miles from Georgetown, Placer county, California, the wife of William George Wilson gave birth to a twelve-pound boy baby. This was the first child born in the camp. Some miner of a jocular disposition at once started the story that Bill Wilson had found a twelve-pound nugget, the handsomest ever seen. The news of Bill's "big find" ran like wild fire up and down the canyon, where hundreds of men were at work. At once there was a grand rush to Bill Wilson's cabin. Every miner was anxious to see the twelve-pound lump.

Bill "dropped on" the joke at once. Taking the men, a few at a time, he introduced them into the room where his living nugget lay and proudly exhibited it as the best and biggest find ever made on Canyon Creek. The joke took at once with the miners. As each squad came out of the cabin every man solemnly asserted that Bill's nugget was the "boss," the finest ever seen. All went away, up and down the creek, spreading the news of the wonderful nugget. The joke was so well kept that the rush to Bill Wilson's cabin continued all day and far into the night. Indeed, the first day did not end the rush. Men came for

Five changes of horses were made on the route. Judge Richard Rising also made a similar trip from Reno to Virginia City, on the buckboard, with Mr. Bennett in 1869, in one hour and seven minutes. These express companies ran in opposition from June, 1868, until December, 1869, during which time the Pacific only came in ahead once by merely a scratch. A race day between the rival companies, whether by coaches, buckboards or ponies, was an occasion of great popular excitement, every body gathering in from Gold Hill, Silver City and all around to witness it. The side walks were lined, telegraph poles climbed, balconies, awnings and house-tops crowded, and all sorts of bets were made, from a thousand dollars in gold coin to a bit drink or a two-bit cigar.

SOME OF THE OLD TIME DRIVERS.

Very few of the original stage drivers remain on the Comstock. Two or three perhaps and scarcely half a dozen are to be found in all Nevada. "Baldy" Green, so called because of a remarkable scarcity of hirsute thatch on the roof of his cranium, drove between Virginia City and Carson on the Overland and other routes in Nevada. "Baldy" is remembered as an unfortunate among the drivers in the matter of encounters with road agents, These gentry seemed to follow "Baldy" like bad luck. Let him go on whatever route he might, his coaches were so often halted and robbed that "Hand down the box, 'Baldy!'" became a standing joke on the Comstock.

"Baldy" thus unwillingly made the acquaintance of "Rattlesnake Dick," Jack Davis and several other noted gentlemen of the highway. Even when "Baldy" got away out in

Idaho, they still found him and ordered him to "hand down the box" as usual, meaning Wells, Fargo & Co.'s treasure box, of course.

Billy Wilson, an old driver and stage proprietor, came over from California in 1860 and started a line of stages between Virginia City and Carson. Before coming over the mountains he owned a stage line between Nevada City and San Juan.

"Big" John Littlefield drove out of Sacramento for years in the early days. Afterward he was on the Henness Pass route. He was a man who weighed about two hundred and fifty pounds. During the war he enlisted and was stationed at Fort Churchill, where he was known as Lietenant Littlefield. He died at Gilroy, California, in 1872.

Miles Nesbit, a driver on the Henness Pass road, was killed at Virginia City in 1866 by the running away of his team. He was thrown from his seat on the coach as it whirled around onto "F" Street, landing on his head, and was taken up dead.

"Curly Bill," William Gearhart, one of the best and most favorably known of the Henness Pass drivers, is now engaged in the livery business in San Francisco.

Billy Hodge, of the same route, is now in the Yosemite Valley.

Cy Hawley killed himself at Lake Tahoe a few years ago.

Johnny Burnett, also of the Henness, killed himself in Denver several years ago.

"Smokey" is now in Reno.

Ned Blair died at Virginia City.

Hank Monk, the famous driver of Horace Greely, died at Carson in 1884.

Pony King, of the Placerville route, died in Carson ten years ago.

Tom Stephens is in San Francisco,

George Emory, also of the Henness, is driving on the Bodie road or at Carson.

E. Douglass, called "Old Dug" for short drove for a time between Virginia City and Reno, also on the Virginia and Gold Hill Bus line. He was in Virginia or San Francisco at last accounts.

Charley Watson, of the Placerville route, is somewhere in California.

John Wilson, of the Henness, died in 1888 at Reno.

Lige Downer, of the Placerville, is somewhere in California.

Frank Henderson, of the Placerville, is now in Canada.

Dye Tyrrell, of the Placerville, is in Colorado. He was for several years Wells, Fargo & Co.'s division agent at Denver.

Charley Livermore, of the Henness, is in Idaho.

Steve Hamon, who in the early days had a stage line between Virginia and Washoe City, died at Elko, recently, of heart disease while seated on the box of his coach.

Jim Dike, an old driver for Langton & Co.'s Express, between Virginia and Marysville, is now in California.

"Bigelow" (Dubois), who drove for Langton & Co. between Virginia and Carson, and who also drove on the Henness, Placerville and Overland routes, is in Virginia or Carson. In the early days of California he drove between Oroville and Dogtown and between Sacramento and Marysville.

Alex McShea was an Overland driver whose present whereabouts are unknown.

"Jim Muggins," otherwise James Lynch, was a driver on Jim McCue's line over the Henness Pass route before the time of the Pacific Express. He died in Oregon twelve years ago.

Ben Billings, who also drove for McCue, and Sam and Billy Russell, who owned the first line of stages between

Virginia and Dayton, are living somewhere in California.

"Dave Red," who drove out of Virginia on the Overland with "Baldy" Green, was drowned some years ago while taking a bath in a pond or reservoir in the neighborhood of Austin, Nevada.

Charley Hainsworth, also an Overland driver, is now agent for Wells, Fargo & Co. on some route leading to Boise City, Idaho.

Charley Stoddard, a Henness driver, who is remembered as the one who upset his coach into the Truckee river, is now somewhere in the Atlantic States.

The one black sheep is Dan Smith, who upset his coach at the foot of the Geiger grade, killing Mrs. Kruttschnitt. He was afterward convicted of mail robbery in Oregon and sent to the penitentiary.

Billy Blackmore, a noted old Henness driver, is now in San Francisco.

W. P. Bennett, for many years in Wells, Fargo & Co,'s employ as driver of stages, buckboards, express wagons, etc., is now employed at the Yellow Jacket mine, Gold Hill.

Owing to the nature of their occupation and their roving unsettled life, it is a difficult matter to keep track of stage drivers. They move from one place to another on the same line. A few more of the old-time drivers might perhaps be searched out, but the foregoing are about all of those who are well remembered by the people of Virginia, San Francisco and sections generally

STAGE LINES OF THE EARLY DAYS.

Among the stage lines in operation in the early days may be mentioned Langton & Co.; Pioneer Express, from Vir-

ginia City to Downieville, San Juan and Marysville, of
which J. S. Albro was the Virginia agent; James McCue's
line by way of Henness Pass; Wells, Fargo & Co., or the
Pioneer Stage line, and the California Stage Co.'s lines by
the Placerville and Henness Pass routes, and several small
transient lines running and branching out in various directions.

Lloyd Rawlings, who was the Virginia agent of the California stage line for some years, is now in Mexico.

Ike Mooney, at first driver and afterwards agent for Langton's Express, is in Sierra county, California, and C. C.
Cooper, who was also agent of the same line for some years
is in California.

Geo. A. Gray, who was Agent and driver for some of the
small lines, died at Virginia about ten years ago.

"Big Jake," who was a driver on the Henness Pass road
in the early days, and a well known sport, is somewhere in
California.

A TERRIFIC DASH DOWN THE SIERRAS.

The trip on which Hank Monk, the famous stage driver of
the Sierras, drove Horace Greely into Placerville has often
been spoken of and made Monk famous, but his greatest
and most dangerous feat was a night dash down the eastern
slope of the Sierras. It was in 1862, and was really a runa-
way of the stage team, though none of the passengers were
aware of the fact. The team ran from the Summit down to
Van Sickle's Station, a distance of five and one-half miles
which distance was made in sixteen minutes. Hank left
the Summit all right. The road was frozen and icy, and an

iron shoe was placed under one of the wheels of the coach, as the brake would have been of little use. Thus all seemed safe in the start. However, the coach had proceeded only a little way down the mountain before the iron shoe slipped out from under the wheel. At once the coach crowded down upon the horses, and this so frightened them that they ran away.

W. P. Bennett, of Wells, Fargo & Co.'s Express, was on the driver's seat with Monk and fully understood the peril of the situation. It was impossible for Monk to hold the team or to bring the frightened animals to a halt. All he could do was to guide the runaways round the curves of the road, and soon he no longer had strength in his hands to do that. He told Mr. Bennett he could no longer guide the team and they must just let the horses go and trust to luck.

At every bend in the road they expected to be hurled down the side of the mountain and be dashed to pieces on the rocks hundreds of feet below. However, the horses had been so often driven over the road that, frightened as they were, they instinctively kept in the right track and at last the coach drew up all safe and sound at Van Sickle's.

In giving Horace Greely his rapid drive down the other side of the mountain to Placerville there was no danger, as Monk had full command of his team all the way. This dash, however, was a life and death affair every foot of the way, and death seemed constantly on the point of winning the game.

On the wild ride down the mountain, a funny incident occurred. One of the passengers was Dan Sheehan, now of Gold Hill. Mr. Sheehan had spent all his life at sea, and for many years had been second mate of various sailing vessels. He was on his first trip in a wheeled craft since his boyhood. Before leaving San Francisco, he had lost much sleep and was greatly fatigued by the first part of the journey. On the Summit he had fallen into a deep sleep, which continued all the way down the mountain. Without waking, he became conscious of a great commotion and of flying along with great rapidity. In his dreams, Sheehan thought himself aboard a vessel on a lee shore in a tremendous storm. First he began to take soundings, and called out, "Fi-i-ve and a ha-alf! Fi-ive and a quarter! Fi-ive!" Then, seeming to be greatly alarmed, he sung out, "Starboard watch on deck; take in sail! Three men take in the mizzen royal, three men take in the main foresail; three men take in the main royal; seven men take in the main topsail." By this time the coach was on level ground, near Van Sickle's and its speed was slackened. Some joker then struck a match and held it under the sleeping sailor's nose. "Hard a starboard!" cried he, "I smell hell ahead!"

On stopping at Van Sickle's to change coaches and horses, the sailor man was so excited and bewildered that he tumbled ashore and went into the station forgetting, and leaving behind, a young lady he had in charge. He was so glad to make port and get ashore that he forgot all about his fellow passengers. For half an hour he had the coach mixed up with a ship.

SOME FAST TRIPS.

ACROSS THE CONTINENT BY PONY, STAGE AND RAILROAD—
A LIVELY RECORD.

In this age of fast travel, when the ocean steamer is surprising the world every little while, and the iron horse is knocking distance into the shade, we are inclined to ask ourselves the question, how did the people of forty years ago get along at all? In looking up some of the records of fast time on the Pacific coast way back in the 50's, we have come to the conclusion that some credit for fast time should be given to the good old stage driver, who in sunshine and storm, through snow and dust, by night and by day, drove through the mountain passes and over their summits, oft through blinding snow drifts when the stoutest hearts were made to waver, and again when old Sol would pour down his rays with a force to make one fear that they were nearing the infernal regions. Interesting narratives could be related by some of the old "Knights of the Whip," as they were termed in early days.

The distance across the great American Continent, between New York and San Francisco, is generally stated at about three thousand miles. The problem in the early days of the California gold discovery and consequent rush of immigration was how to travel, or be transported, across or around that intervening space in the shortest time and easiest manner. Many were longer going overland than others who came the seventeen thousand miles around Cape Horn. The hardships encountered by those who made the overland trip are well recorded in the following lines:

CROSSING THE PLAINS IN "49."

In years long since past, when this land of my dreams
Was gained through the hardships of crossing the plains,
When none but the boldest and most daring heart
E'er thought for a moment of taking a part
In the trials and troubles which then did beset

Emigrants striving o'er this journey to get,
When danger and suffering ever was rife,
And many brave fellows had given their life
To the unerring aim of the savage that lay
Awaiting the victims who chanced in his way.
His knife and his tomahawk seldom at rest,
Made those tribes of the forest a terrible pest;
And none suffered more at their hands, for a time,
Than the old pioneers of the year Forty-nine.
Many yet live who can most truly relate
The saddened misfortune and terrible fate
Of many companions whose lifeless remains
Lie buried far off on the desolate plains.
And many's the tear that in vain has been shed,
In hopes that some loved one would safely be led
Through the fierce blinding storm, so bitter and cold,
To the land from which came the promise of gold.
But the demon of death, grim visaged and cold,
Was sure of his victim, and called to his fold
Many brave spirits which in Heaven now shine,
Who died on the plains in the year Forty-nine.
'Twas late in December, of that memorable year,
A small band set off for the western frontier;
Their train was well stocked, as from home they departed,
No fears filled their bosoms, so boldly they started;
No fear of the terrible suffering in store
For that little band as they crossed the plains o'er.
Used to the forest and life in the wildwood,
In which they had lived from the days of their childhood,
They feared not the danger that ever was near
Those crossing the plains at that time o' the year.
Two weeks had but passed since their journey begun,
And many long miles were between them and home.
Still each one was happy and joyful the while,

For good fortune had not ceased upon them to smile.
No accident happened to fill them with sorrow,
No fears made them dread the coming to-morrow.
As at night 'round their blazing camp fires they sat,
Engaged in a pleasant and sociable chat,
Rehearsing the most daring deeds of their life,
For that little band were not strangers to strife,
They could hear, now and then, a fierce hungry cry
Of a stray prowling wolf that was passing near by.
And oft in the darkness and stillness of night,
When wrapped in their blankets so snug and so tight,
The unwelcome sound of a rifle would tell
That some cunning savage had tracked them too well.
And many's the skirmish they had with the foe
While wading knee deep through the fierce drifting snow.
Those hearts, that at first were so merry and glad,
Were beginning now to grow weary and sad.
The journey was long and the weather severe,
And thoughts of starvation now filled them with fear.
Supplies near exhausted, no prospects ahead
By which their fond hopes of success might be fed.
And some of those brave hearts ne'er strangers to fear,
Were hanging their heads in seeming dispar;
Made willing by hunger and cold to be left
To perish alone by the side of a drift.
And among them was one whose features and form
Told plainly she never could weather the storm.
One night as the little band pitched camp to rest,
Her spirit was called to the land of the blest.
They dug her a grave 'neath a tall forest pine,
And there she has slept since the year Forty-nine.
The storm had soon ceased and the sun brightly rose
And shone on the grave where in death did repose
The first fair victim who at eve used to cheer

That wandering band with some favorite air.
That sweet loving voice they would ne'er hear again,
'Twas hushed in the stillness far out on the plain.
At last the bright land of their hopes did appear,
And as they crossed over its welcome frontier,
What joy filled their hearts as they knelt down in prayer
And thanked the Almighty for guiding them there.
For when dark despair had baffled all hope,
And struggles seemed vain in those woods so remote,
He cast o'er the scene a bright halo of light,
And shielded them oft in the terrible fight.
All those old pioneers who should chance to peruse
These few simple lines from the pen of the muse,
I ask thee in truth if the scenes I portray
Are not truthful scenes of that early day;
And if emigrants had not a terrible time
Crossing over the plains in the year Forty-nine.

The demand for speedier travel, transportation and mail facilities became a naturally pressing result, and the month or two occupied in transit by way of Panama or Nicaragua was considered inadequate. Railroad communication from the east to the Missouri river was already progressing and speedily established, and the overland stage line and pony express soon distanced the Isthmus route.

The trans-continental railroad subsequently reduced the time to about one week, and the occupation of the stages and ponies was gone. The pony express made it in nine days, before the telegraph reduced it to nine or ten seconds.

But a record of some of the fast time made in trips across the continent in those early days, considering the innumerable and extensive difficulties that had to be encountered, furnishing matter as it does for a most interesting book for

the readers of the present day. The pony and stage sta-
tions were established at the most convenient and practi-
cable points and distances, and the very best horses obtain-
able were brought into service. The roads were new and
the numerous rivers and creeks had to be crossed by ford-
ing, swimming or in scows, on rafts or other primitive ar-
rangements before regular bridges could be constructed.
Hostile Indians was not the least one of the troubles to be
encountered, and their interference with the progress of the
emigrant in his long and wearisome journey was at times
almost unbearable. Considering all the difficulties which
had to be surmounted in making the numerous connections,
the success and good time made by the pony express and
the stage and railroad combination from St. Louis, Mo., to
Folsom, California, was really wonderful, even as compared
with the through railroad transit of the present day. In
1861 the trip was made from New York to San Francisco
in nine days, or two hundred and sixteen hours—over
thirteen miles per hour. In 1862 it was made in seven
days or 168 hours—over seventeen miles per hour. Ben
Holliday's trip in 1862 from San Francisco to New York was
made in ten days or 240 hours—12½ miles per hour. In
1864, Messrs. Skae and Lent made a trip from Virginia City
to Sacramento, 158 miles, in twelves hours and twenty minutes, carried by the Pioneer Stage Company. In 1865,
Louis McLane and daughter made the trip from San Francisco to New York, by steamboat, stage and railroad,
across the continent in eight days, or 192 hours—over
fifteen miles per hour- distance, 3,000 miles.

In 1875, the same trip was made by rail in seven days, or
168 hours—nearly eighteen miles per hour.

In 1889, it was made by rail in five days, or 120 hours—
twenty-five miles per hour.

In 1890, it was made by rail in about four and one-half

days, or at the rate of twenty-seven miles per hour..

OVER THE MOUNTAINS.

It is in the fast trips across the Sierra mountains, that the old "Knights of the Whip," those who are still clinging to this mundane sphere, love to talk about and ponder over, and why should they not do so, for those were days in which men's souls were tried and their physical abilities severely tested. Some of those fast trips which are recorded in the early history of California and Nevada, have caused many a mind to wonder how it was possible for any mortal handling the lines of a six in-hand, to, I might say, almost fly down the steep and rocky canyons of the Sierras without being dashed into eternity. But those drivers were men of great nerve, the occasion required it, and no timid driver was ever sought after by those men who were building up this great western empire.

The ruling spirits in those days, the Hollidays, the McLanes, the Lents, the Skaes, the Stanfords and the Crockers were men who could not stop at any obstacle. Favored by the Almighty with a spirit of enterprise and the opportunities at hand for the carrying of it out, they proved themselves the right men in the right place, and the people of the Pacific coast today owe to these men a debt of gratitude for laying the foundation of this great and prosperous section of our country. Speaking of fast trips across the Sierra Nevadas, might be mentioned one made by Ben Holliday and Chas. McLane in 1862. Starting from Folsom, California, they reached Carson City, Nevada, 122 miles, in ten and one-half hours, including stoppages--9½ hours traveling time. When we consider the nature of the country over which they had to ride, the steep grades and poorly made roads, we are compelled to admit that Mr. Wm. P. Bennett, who drove the stage on that occasion, was no amateur in the business.

One of the most exciting trips in the line of staging over the Sierra Nevada mountains in the early days, was the one which Charles Crocker and Wm. Hamilton made from Sacramento to Virginia City in 1864. They were representing the California Stage Company and were doing every-thing that money and brains could accomplish to distance the record of Wells, Fargo & Co. Money was no object at all and the very finest of stock was secured that the great end of fast time might be accomplished. Starting from Sac-ramento, the two set out on their tedious journey over the mountains, changing horses every twelve miles. "Get there on time" was the standing order of the company and they did get there about five minutes ahead of Wells, Fargo's time, but at a cost of many thousand dollars for some twelve of their fine horses were put hors de combat—unfit for fut-ure use. I would here state that the time made was 12 hour and 18 minutes for 158 miles, but when we consider the difference in distance of railroad travel of each company, we find that Wells, Fargo's time was not beaten.

In 1869 there were lively times upon the road from Reno to Virginia City, for at that time rival express companies existed, and horse flesh was by no means spared by those companies who were anxious to out-run each other, and go down into history with a world-surprising record.

The distance over this road from Reno to Virginia City was twenty-two miles, and the quickest time made by the ponies, under saddle, was fifty-eight minutes. The time made by a two-horse buckboard was sixty-five minutes. This time, considering the grade, is unprecedented. The latter part, or home stretch, of this wild racing was up and over the steep Geiger Grade, from Steamboat Valley about ten miles, into Virginia City, the summit of the grade being over 2,000 feet above the valley.

In all such contests for high speed pressure racing, plenty of good horses were provided, regardless of expense, and the relays were frequent, but it required very active work and keen watchfullness on the part of the station men, riders and drivers. Faster time is seldom heard of or recorded in history.

GOING INTO PLACERVILLE IN '49.

(SEE PICTURE NO. 1.)

Placerville, known as "Hangtown" in the "days of '49" was the first of the mining camps reached by those who came to California across the plains. All hailed old "Hangtown" with joy, for on reaching that place they felt that the thirst, alkali desert, Indian murderers and all the other terrors of the overland wilds had been left behind. At Placerville were found some wonderfully rich diggings, and there the emigrant, greedy for gold, saw for the first time in his life mines of the yellow metal. They rush in like wild men, and indeed they are men wild with hunger for gold. Each man expects it will be his luck to find in some secret nook in the mountains a spot where he will take out gold by the pound. Such has been his dream during all the long weary days and nights on the plains.

Of course, among the new arrivals in the camp are greedy fellows ready to rush in, stake out and claim all the mining ground in sight, but all such meet with a rebuff in the very start. Conspiciously posted up about the diggings they see notices in large letters reading: "No

man shall hold more than one claim." All must
submit to this, for it is the law of the camp, and there
are plenty of revolvers ready to sustain the law. All at
work in the mines are law abiding men. The laws are not
many. All the laws of the place may easily be rolled up
in a small wad and fired into a man from the muzzle of a
revolver. Every miner in the camp is a good interpreter of
the law and is sound in regard to the gospel of the diggings.

The name "Hangtown" was given to the camp because
of the many men hanged there in the early days by order
of the court of "Judge Lynch." An oak tree that stood
where Coloma street now runs, often bore "other green
fruit" than acorns in the days of '49. Many a desperado
then "danced in the air." At one time this oak was as well
known and as much dreaded by roughs as was the famous
cottonwood tree on Cherry Creek, Denver, Colorado.

In the spring of 1850, Placerville grew like a mush-
room. Stores, dwellings, hotels, saloons and gambling dens appeared as if by magic. Scores of
buildings were seen going up in all directions at the
same moment and tents dotted all the suburbs. Gamblers and sharpers of all kinds flocked to the town to meet
the long emigrant trains that came rolling in across the
plains. Bands of music were playing in all the big gambling
houses and leading saloons, and the town was at fever-heat,
both day and night.

Emigrants, on their first arrival in the place, felt as though
they had landed in a genuine "Vanity Fair," the town being
constantly in a state of bewildering uproar. Men were
shouting out all manner of offers or telling of wonderful at-
tractions on every street and corner. There seemed no end
of wealth flying about. On Sundays, hundreds of miners
came up from the river and down from the creeks and

gulches and then the town was a veritable pandemonium. Among the miners, Sunday was the great day for selling gold dust, and buying provisions and other supplies; also for gambling, drinking and fighting. It was, besides, the day for getting news from all surrounding and outlying camps, and even from distant parts of the country. Wonderful were the stories told of big strikes made in various directions. There were reports of mountains on the sides of which chunks of gold like boulders had been seen sticking out of the ground; and of lakes whose shores were composed of golden sands.

Many a miner deserted diggings that were paying him an ounce a day to go on a wild-goose chase at the time of the "Gold Lake excitement," and there were many other equally wild rushes. Being wholly ignorant of the possibilities of the gold fields of the Sierras, men were in the early days ready to give credit to almost any story that was told. Mountains having in their sides great ribs of gold, did not seem to them impossible, for the majority of miners firmly believe that sooner or later a place would be found where great lumps of pure gold would be seen lying about on the surface of the ground. This place was always supposed to be situated somewhere high in the wilds of the mountains.

Such stories told to gold-greedy emigrants, who arrived in the country barefoot, ragged and "dead broke," set them wild. They were ready to sell horses, oxen, wagons and all else for a song, and rush away to the new digging where they could gather gold dust by the pound, and nuggets by the peck.

The main emigrant road over the Sierras forked at Slippery Ford, above Strawberry, one branch going to "Hangtown" and the other to Georgetown. Many men working in the mines lower down came up to those two towns to meet friends expected in across the plains on purpose to guard and protect them from the swindlers lying in wait at these notorious advance posts to rob them of their property. The interference of these honest miners with the schemes of the thieves and swindlers not unfrequently resulted in giving the incoming immigrants their first view of a real red-hot pistol fight, or a genuine, well-conducted "neck-tie party."

Placerville is now a quiet and beautiful little town as is to be found in the mountains. It is embowered in orchards and vineyards, and in it peaceful and industrious people make their homes. In passing along its pleasant streets today, it is difficult to realize the wild and fearful scenes enacted there only a few years ago.

GEORGETOWN IN '50. (SEE PICTURE NO. 2.)

RAPID GROWTH OF THE TOWN—STREET SCENES—A BALL IN THE DIGGINGS.

Georgetown contained only six cabins in the spring of 1849, but in the spring of 1850 there was a regular building mania. Stores, dwellings, saloons and cabins seemed to spring out of the ground in a single night. On all sides were heard the sounds of the hammer and the saw. All who wished to build, staked out and helped themselves to whatever ground they wanted, as for a time building lots were to be had without money and without price.

Many began business in the open air without waiting to build.

The biggest saloon in the town was in a tent. The tent was almost as large as an ordinary circus canvas. In this

great tent no fewer than eight gambling tables were running at the same time and two bands of music were in full
blast.

Besides the big tent, there were in the town several other
places in which faro games were running both day and
night. In addition to all these games, three-card Monte,
poker, thimble-rig, the strap game and all manner of
other games were to be seen in progress in the streets.
Every big pine stump in the main street was utilized as a
gambling table.

Sunday was the day when all the games were liveliest,
as then the miners came in from all the gulches with big
buckskin bags filled with gold dust, ounces of which they
staked on a single card. In the midst of all the drinking,
gambling and fighting an itinerant preacher, mounted upon
a stump was often to be seen holding forth, fighting the
devil in his very den. Though these preachers soundly
lashed their hearers right and left, they were not only re-
spectfully listened to, but were also very liberally re-
warded. When the hat was passed around it did not become a receptacle of smooth dimes, rusty coppers and old
buttons, as is often the case in more settled and civilized
communities in these degenerate days; on the contrary, the
hat was well loaded down with gold and silver, not a few
miners throwing in it "chispas" worth $5 and $10, and now
and again a nugget of an ounce or two was dropped into
the preacher's "grab-bag."

FIRST APPEARANCE OF JUDGE LYNCH.

In the autumn of 1850, Georgetown had its first hanging.
It was an affair of the people. John Williams, a miner from
Australia, shot and killed his wife in a fit of jealousy. It
was a very cold-blooded affair. News of the murder spread
rapidly. Soon there was heard up and down the river a

loud and peculiar whooping. It was the gathering signal of the miners. Yell answered yell, echoing far up and down among the mountains. It was a call that all were bound to obey. In a short time four or five hundred miners had collected. They marched in a body to Georgetown and demanded Williams of the sheriff. The officer refused to give up his prisoner. The miners then cut down two or three young pines and of the trunks constructed a battering ram. In less than ten minutes the jail was demolished.

When the citizens had secured the murderer, they placed a rope about his neck and led him to a big pine tree. The end of the rope was thrown over a convenient limb, when a mule was brought and Williams hoisted upon the animal's back. There was on the back of the mule a Mexican pack-saddle. Williams was told to kneel on the saddle and make his peace with God. When he had finished his prayer, the murderer was ordered to stand up. He obeyed, and when he was on his feet some one gave the mule a sharp cut with a whip. The animal gave a bound and the wife-murderer was left dangling in the air. He fell about the regulation distance and in four or five minutes life was extinct. Having executed this piece of summary justice, the miners immediately dispersed and resumed work in their several claims, leaving behind them a very quiet town.

GAMBLING IN PLACERVILLE.

(SEE PICTURE NO. 3.)

No, not all were rugged miners,
   In the noted days of yore,
When the famed banks of Yuba
   For gold men did explore.
There was found a class of people

Who wore fine clothes, and such
A hatred had lor labor
That a pick they'd never touch.

Those men lived a life of pleasure,
  They gambled day and night,
They were always quiet and sober
  And ne'er provoked a fight;
Still the demon dwelt within them
  And provoked, danger then was near,
For gamblers in those early days
  Knew no such word as fear.

Good old Placerville was noted
  For the free and easy way,
Some "old boys" their time devoted
  To make the "diggins" pay.
Little used to manual labor,
  They were all wide awake,
The cards they well could shuffle
  And the dice could nicely shake.

One glance at this noted picture
  Shows the gamblers all arrayed
In garments the most stylish,
  By some custom tailor made.
See the plain and honest miner,
  Standing by in deep surprise,
Watching every single jesture
  Of the well dressed "boys."

He, perhaps, has lost his money
  Betting on the jack or four,
And he leaves the quarters scowling,
  His feelings they are sore.
For good luck it went against him
  And he felt it was a "bust,"

And he went his way lamenting
The loss of all his dust.

Temptation oft would urge them
To try their luck in chance,
And to the treacherous card table
They would slowly then advance.
You could see it in their manner
That they felt out of place,
For the thoughts of home and loved ones
In their bosoms they could trace.

In the doorway stands a mother
Gazing in upon the crowd,
And perhaps it is her husband
She hears talking now so loud;
By her side her little offspring
Calling to his pa to come.
Such scenes as this, dear reader,
Many a woman's bosom wrung.

Ah! those pioneers were generous,
They were God's noblest work;
They reared from out a wilderness
A country which now shows forth
As the grandest and the richest
Beneath the glorious sun.
Yes, and all through toil and valor
Were those enduring blessings won.

SUNDAY IN THE MINER'S CABIN.

(SEE PICTURE NO. 4.)

Sunday was not a day of rest in the mines, though a day
of cessation from the toil of mining. Sunday was the day for
attending to all the small jobs of work and household and

other duties left to care for themselves during the week. It was a day of washing, mending, bread-baking and letter-writing. On that day were forced upon the miner recollections of the domestic arts which he had seen practiced in his youth—in the days when he thought his old mother was a little "cranky" when she declared that "a woman's work is never done." Now he sees how disagreeable was much of that work, as, bending over his wash-tub, he drops a soapy tear at the thought of his old mother still toiling slavishly about the old double-log cabin back in "Pike County," or some other region in the States east of the Rockies.

While one man is fuming and sputtering over the wash-tub, another penitent sinner, who in times of old thought the work of woman mere play, is bunglingly patching the seat of his unmentionables with a piece of "self-rising" flour sack. He sighs as he thinks of the little woman away down East who was wont, in times past, to gather up his "old duds" and put in the "stitch in time"—he sighs, for he now remembers that he never once thought to thank her for her pains; he will have a better appreciation of woman's work when he gets home. Mayhap, however, he never reached home—his bones may have been left to bleach in some wild canyon. Who knows?

While some are engaged in these and similar domestic occupations, others are writing letters home, and perhaps two or more are amusing themselves at a game of bean-poker. Some one will presently go to the post office and on his return, if a steamer has just got in, there will be a good time at reading home papers and letters.

THE MASSACRE AT MURDERERS' BAR.

(SEE PICTURE NO. 5.)

A memorable affair in the early history of gold mining in

California was the massacre of white miners at Murderers'
Bar, below Coloma, on the South Fork of the American
river, in October, 1849. There were twenty-three men at
work on the bar, eighteen of whom were killed on the spot
and one was so badly wounded that he survived but a short
time. The Indians in overwhelming numbers boldly made
their appearance in broad daylight. They were armed
with bows and arrows, also carried spears, or lances, on the
heads of which were fixed sharp points of flint or obsidian,
similar to those on their arrows, but much longer and
broader. The Indians made a sudden rush around a rocky
point while the men were at work, and getting between
them and the camp where their arms were stored, killed,
in a few minutes, all except four men on the opposite side
of the river. These men were operating in the bottom of
the river by means of an India rubber diving dress or
submarine armor. At the time the Indians made their rush,
one of the four men was in the diving dress down under
water working in a crevice, while the others were above,
pumping air down to him. The men above signalled the
diver to come up. As he rose to the surface in his armor
and turned his head with its great glass eyes toward the
opposite shore, the Indians caught sight of him. At the
same moment, a jackass that was tied in a clump of bushes
began braying. At sight of the frightful specter that came
up out of the bed of the river, and on hearing the awful
whoops it was supposed to be uttering, a howl of terror
arose among the Indians and all fled precipitately from the
spot. Not a gun, knife, blanket or single piece of property
of any kind was taken by the savages. When the big-eyed
monster came up out of the water, all turned tail and fled
in dismay. The Indians evidently believed that what they
saw was some mighty avenging water devil that was about to
charge into their midst, as not one of the tribe was ever

again seen on the bar. Even as late as 1861, no Digger Indians could be induced to go near that part of the river in which the big-eyed devil was supposed to dwell.

SAW THE ELEPHANT.

(SEE PICTURE NO. 6.)

The grizzly bear is now given the place of honor among the beasts of California as the "monarch of the Sierras." In the days of '49, however, the elephant was king in California. The new-comer was a "green horn" until after he had seen the elephant. The beast was not hard to find. He ranged as often in the big towns of the valleys as in the mountain mining camps. He assumed all manner of shapes and disguises, hiding his tusks and trunk in order to make sure of his intended victims, and it was not until too late that the man found he had encountered that mighty beast, the elephant. At times he appeared as the "gentle gazelle," then, perhaps, as the faithful dog, "Trusty," and again as the stupid donkey, and the victim never once suspected the true character of the beast with which he had to do, until he found himself completely flattened out under its huge feet; when to his astonished gaze appeared trunk, tail and tusks, and he knew he had "seen the elephant." The elephant was not a profitable beast to see. Under the pressure of his huge bulk, the buckskin bag of the honest miner was always completely flattened out. A single sight of the elephant at the Bay sent many a man back to the mountains, when he had confidently expected to be "sailing the salt seas," homeward bound. The elephant, whose haunt was at and about the bay, was an immense beast, and old Satan himself was not more cunning. A man might for years escape the mountain elephant only to fall a victim to the

terrible beast that ranged down at tide water. One good
view of the elephant in any one of the many shapes he assumed generally thoroughly satisfied all sensible men, but
there were those who, after their first introduction, became
confirmed elephant hunters. There seemed to be a sort of
fascination for them about the mighty beast and they were
always following his trail. The bones of these infatuated
men are strewn from the summit of the Sierras to the shores
of the sea. In the days of old, a man had only to say, "I
have seen the elephant," to let it be known that he had
been "through the mills" and had come out pretty thoroughly pulverized.

A "HOOP UP" IN CAMP.

(SEE PICTURE NO. 7.)

In 1849, a store-keeper in Nevada City brought up from
Sacramento a few hooped skirts, as women were then beginning to arrive in the town. About the time the skirts
arrived, some of the miners of the outlaying camp of Deer
Creek came down to town after supplies. A young fellow
of the party, who was full of fun, bought one of the skirts
and took it up to the camp on Deer Creek. The men up
there had not seen a woman for so long that even a bit of
feminine gear was a novelty to them. The young fellow
put on his skirt and with it all manner of girlish airs. His
mimicry excited shouts of laughter and a fiddle being procured, every man in the camp had to have a dance with
him. The thing was so ludicrous that all hands got on a big
spree and "hooped it up" half the night, cheered on by the
man behind the bar, who was raking in gold dust without
stint, and half the time without either weight or measure.

The next day the skirt was hung outside of the cabin of

the owner. As it dangled there in the breeze, it caught the sight of every man who came down from diggings higher up the creek. The man would stop as if shot. Having assured himself that his eyes did not deceive him, the newcomer would then saunter down to the saloon and, after having taken a "nip," would, in a careless sort of way, ask about the woman who had come to the camp. Being caught, he would then feel it his duty to treat all hands That skirt proved the best sign for the saloon-keeper that could possibly have been invented It brought him in many an ounce of good Deer Creek gold dust.

THE LITTLE JOKER IN '49.

(SEE PICTURE NO. 8.)

Here you see one of the phases
  In the bold miner's life,
For a love of strange adventure
  E'er in his heart was rife,
When the prospects were not cheering
  And idle moments came,
Oh! the thoughts of home and pleasures
  Brought thoughts of many a game.

Who could blame those men of valor
  Who dangers great had dared,
If in their few idle moments
  They in chance games had shared.
See, the little "Joker's" booming,
  The betting's somewhat brisk,
For the good old Forty-niner
  Would not stop at any risk,

Oft a rogue would show his col is

And "beat" his comrades bad
In a game that here is pictured
　　Where the joker looks so glad.
When such fellows were discovered
　　The atmosphere grew hot,
And did they not quickly leave the camp
　　They would be hung or shot.

Missouri Bill a feature was
　　In every mining camp,
And where "diggins" were the liveliest
　　'Twas there that Bill would tramp.
True sample of a rustic lord
　　With good and honest will,
None could ever say a word
　　Against Missouri Bill.

MINING ON THE YUBA.

(SEE PICTURE NO. 9.)

A scene like this could oft be found;
A pocket loaded in the ground.
Ah! "struck it rich," this phrase had grown
In every camp to be well known.
Right here you see, with pick in hand,
A miner in amazement stands.
Oh! he has struck it rich, you bet,
While others have it yet to get.
Big nuggets by the score are found
Scattered quite freely o'er the ground.
Among the rocks in outway places,
The sharp miner gold now traces;
Settles down with pan and rocker,
Crying, "boys, I guess we've got her."

This choice scene your eyes now scan,
Might be called here, "Yuba dam."

MAJ. DOWNIE GOING INTO DOWNIEVILLE IN '49.

(SEE PICTURE NO. 10.)

Downieville, Sierra County, was, in the early days, one of the richest placer-mining camps in California. It is still a live mining town, but at the present time is more celebrated for its rich veins of gold-bearing quartz and for the fine drift diggings in its neighborhood than for its remaining placers. The town was named in honor of Major Downie, its founder and one of its first settlers. All old miners love to tell of the wonders of Downieville in its palmy days. There were located the famous "Tin-cup" diggings, where the partners every evening divided their gold by measuring it out in a tin cup of the ordinary size. Above the town a short distance were the celebrated Blue Banks, a deposit of blue gravel that was all alive and sparkling with spangles of gold, and still above these diggings, in the North Fork of the Yuba, at the mouth of Sailor Revine, was dug out the biggest lump of pure gold ever found in California. It was a wonderful camp; there was gold everywhere. The river bars were all full of gold as were all the gulches and ravines and there was gold in the flats, on the hills and deep in the great gravel mountains, with an immense number of rich quartz veins. Major Downie, the pioneer of the camp, was a native of Cleveland, Ohio. At one time he sailed a vessel on Lake Erie, as captain and owner. He then went to Canada and established a store. Several years after he returned to the United States and landed at Buffalo, N. Y., just when news was received of the discovery of gold

in California.   He went aboard a packet boat that very night
and was not again seen by any one who knew him until his
feet were planted on the golden soil of California. Two
men who went to the theater with Major Downie the night
he left Buffalo, and who were the persons last seen with
him, as he lunched at a restaurant after the play, came near
getting into serious trouble on account of his sudden disap-
pearance, for he told no one where he was going.   Luckily
the two men were able to give a good account of themselves
and to find friends to substantiate their statements.

Although thousands made fortunes in the mines at Downieville, the finder of them and the founder of the town re-
mained poor; a freak of fortune of which California affords
hundreds of instances.

THE SPOT WHERE GOLD WAS FIRST FOUND.

(SEE PICTURE NO. II.)

Picture No. 11 depicts the spot where gold was first discovered in 1848, at Sutter's sawmill, on the American river.
Here now stands the town of Coloma. The history of the
finding of the first gold by Marshall and his party of mill-
builders has been so often written and is so familiar that it
need not be here repeated. The picture shows the place
after the discovery had been made and after Indians had
been employed in the work of searching for the precious
nuggets.   The twin pine trees will at once be recognized by
all who have ever visited Coloma. These two trees have
looked down upon some exciting scenes. The first nugget
found is now the property of the wife of Peter Wimmer, a
millwright who was at work on the saw-mill that was being
built by Colonel Sutter. Plenty of thin scales of gold had
been seen before the nugget was found, but they were sup-

posed to be scales of mica.

Mrs. Wimmer was a Georgia woman and had often seen placer gold in her native State. She at once pronounced the nugget gold. To prove what she asserted and to show that the metal would not tarnish, she put it into her soap kettle (she was making soft soap at the time) and boiled it for several hours. This first nugget is now in the keeping of a member of the Society of Pacific Coast Pioneers, at San Francisco, but still belongs to Mrs. Wimmer. It is about an inch long, is quite thin at the edges and is somewhat rough in places. It is worth $5.05.

Marshall was superintending the erection of the mill and got the credit of finding the first gold, but the men had seen scales of gold shining among the gravel in the tail-race for two or three days before the nugget was found. There was talk among the men at table about the glittering scales before Mrs. Wimmer, who kept the boarding house at the sawmill, and remembering her old Georgia home, she said the little scales mentioned must be gold. Marshall scouted the idea, saying the scales were mica. He would not believe that the shining stuff was gold even after a piece big enough to be tested by Mrs. Wimmer had been found. He was ashamed to go down to Sutter's Fort with the bit of metal and wanted Wimmer to take it. Wimmer was willing to go, but at the last moment could not find his horse. Marshall then offered his horse but Wimmer was afraid to ride it. At last Marshall consented to take the "find" to the Fort for a scientific test. He went, however, with many doubts and misgivings, fearing he would be laughed at. The specimen stood all tests, was pronounced genuine gold, and then began the boom in mining, which has not yet ended. Millions untold still lie in the soil and the quartz veins of California.

SILAS HAIGHT'S FAMOUS BEAR FIGHT.

(SEE PICTURE NO. 12.)

Cub Canyon, El Dorado county, California, received its name from a memorable battle had there in 1852, by Silas Haight, with a grizzly bear. The bear was a she one with two cubs. Silas was passing down the canyon, when a sharp bend in the trail brought him face to face with the old bear. A log lay across the steep and slippery trail and against this Silas brought up just as the bear was in the act of climbing it. The mother bear at once clasped Silas with her claws, the cubs keeping close behind her and setting up a hungry whine.

Mr. Haight had a gun on his shoulders, but was engaged at too close quarters to use it. While he was trying to bring his gun to bear upon the old grizzly, she had one paw around his head and was cuffing and tearing at him with the other. Finally she pulled Silas over the log, when man and bear had it in regular rough-and-tumble fashion for a time on the ground.

Silas had about made up his mind that the bear would win the fight, when a fresh outbreak of whining on the part of the cubs caused the mother to turn her head to look after them. In a moment the man was on his feet and so, too, was the bear. As the bear came at Silas he tried to raise his gun (which he had taken off the ground on getting up) to use it as a club, but the bear siezed it in her mouth and took it from him, at the same time striking him a blow that broke his right arm.

Drawing his bowie knife with his left hand, Silas then closed in on the bear and began stabbing her. As she all the time kept the gun in her mouth she was unable to bite, but she still fought savagely with her terrible claws. At last Silas' long knife reached the heart of the infuriated

beast and she fell dead. Silas was but little better than a
dead man when he gained the victory. The bear had torn
away one of his ears with the scalp on that side and the
same blow had crushed in his skull and broken his jaw.
One of his legs was also disabled, yet he managed to crawl
a distance of two miles to where he obtained assistance and
medical attendance.

Contrary to the predictions of all who saw him, Silas recovered from his fearful injuries and after a long time what
was left of him was able to crawl about. He wore a large
silver plate on his skull, and was always lame in one leg.
Silas had his ear, a large piece of scalp and three fingers
that had been bitten off his right hand in the fight, pre-
served in alcohol. These fragments of himself he carried
about in a bottle, as he went from camp to camp seek-
ing assistance to take him to his old home in the East.

Silas Haight was a native of Illinois. After his recov-
ery, he lived the greater part of the time about Yankee
Jim's, Todd's Valley and Michigan Bluffs, but visited every mining camp of note in the country, traveling about
and exhibiting his "remains," living and dead, for over
a year. Everywhere the compassionate and charitable gold
diggers brought forth their buckskin sacks and poured into his hand a generous gift of dust, for his appearance and
the "credentials" he carried in his bottle showed that he
was no imposter. What was lacking from the man's anat-
omy was to be seen in the bottle, and no one could doubt
when the unfortunate was able to show that he could recon
struct himself from the materials on hand. In a little over
a year, Silas received eight or ten thousand dollars, as was
supposed. No one ever knew, as Silas was shrewd in some
things, but before leaving for home he acknowledged that
he had money enough to buy a good farm in Illinois, and
to make himself comfortable for the remainder of his life.

Silas never had any use of his right arm and but little use of his lame leg. A curious phenomenon in his case was that he was always a little "flighty" at every change of the moon, and a singular circumstance in connection with his temporary mental derangement was that he saw bears all about him. Big and little bears were coming for him from all quarters and were clambering, waltzing and tumbling all about him. His brain was not so far disordered as to render him violent at such times. He knew that the bears were mere phantoms, yet he could not prevent their coming. One-half of his brain saw the bears while the othe —the sound half—told him that they were mere shadows.

When Silas had crawled down to the nearest camp after his victory, some men went up the canyon to the scene of the fight. They found the two cubs whining over their dead mother and licking her many wounds. The cubs were captured without trouble, as they were quite small. These men found at the log that lay across the canyon, below it and all about, ample evidence of the terrible battle that had taken place at the spot; also found Haight's gun with the stock badly chewed up. Silas Haight's bear fight was the most desperate affair of the kind ever known in California.

ON THE PLAINS IN "49."

(SEE PICTURE NO. 14.)

Volumes have been written descriptive of the hardships and perils encountered by those who crossed the plains during the first years of the California gold excitement. It is not intended here to enter into an account of what was endured by those early emigrants, but merely to give one or two incidents and facts not so widely known as the

main story of the grand exodus. Many stories have been
told of troubles with the Indians, but one of the most curious is the following: On one occasion a train of seven wagons had camped together when half a dozen Indians rode
up. They scattered themselves among the wagons and began begging and bartering. A young man belonging to one
of the wagons had a very handsome wife. To plague her,
the husband pretended to an Indian that he wanted to trade
her off. He said he would give her for the pony on which
the Indian was mounted. The Indian took the offer in
good faith and said it was a bargain. Finally, when the
brave found he was only being fooled with and laughed at,
he threw his lasso and caught the young wife about the
waist. He then gave his war-whoop and dashed off with
her. As the woman was being dragged away, a man
picked up a gun and shot the Indian's pony. Drawing his revolver he then ran up and shot the Indian dead. On being
released, the woman was found to be considerably bruised,
but her injuries were not of a serious nature. The only
regret felt by the party was that the Indian had not lassoed
and dragged the silly husband. When their companion
was killed the other Indians at once mounted their ponies
and dashed away. For several days and nights the emigrant party were in constant dread of an attack by the
Indians, but they saw them no more. Perhaps, however,
the Indians avenged themselves by murdering some weaker
party.

All have heard of the hand-cart and wheel-barrow men
who crossed the plains, but the history of the two men
who first started out in that way is not so well known, as
they wheeled their craft no farther than Salt Lake. It ap-
pears that a year before, Brigham Young had predicted that
Gentiles would yet be seen coming to Zion with hand-carts
and wheelbarrows. The wheelbarrow man had abandoned

his craft 100 miles back, and the man with the hand cart had given up when still forty miles from Salt Lake City. The Mormons were so delighted that Brigham's prediction had been fulfilled, or nearly so, that they hired the two men to go back and bring in their vehicles. The wheelbarrow man was made a present of $200 in gold when he came wheeling into Salt Lake, and the man of the hand cart received $100 in gold coin.

The Mormons then boasted greatly of the fulfillment of the words of their prophet, but the Gentiles all saw Brigham's hand in the affair. Afterward several men went all the way to California with both wheelbarrows and hand carts.

THE HUMBOLDT DESERT.

To all who crossed the plains in the early days, the Humboldt desert was a great terror. It is a vast, waterless waste of sand and alkali. No living creature makes its home in the Humboldt desert, nor is any green thing to be found within its borders. It is a region of thirst, mirages and whirling pillars of sand. On this great sea of sand, in the early days, many emigrant families were cast away and hundreds of head of cattle and horses perished. It was the last and greatest peril to be passed before entering the promised golden land. The misery of it was that this burning and waterless region had to be encountered with horses and oxen that were exhausted by the toil and was reduced to skeletons by the privations of many weary weeks of previous travel in the wilderness. Therefore that the desert came in almost at the end of the journey made it all the more dangerous and fatal. Hundreds of wagons were abandoned because of the dying of the animals that vainly strove to drag them through the hot and yielding sands. Many

men as well as animals perished in this dismal desert—
lay down and died almost in sight of the promised land.

John R. Ridge, the Cherokee Indian chief and poet, who
died only a few years ago at his home in Grass Valley, California, has well portrayed the terrors of the Humboldt desert.
What he wrote of, he saw as an emigrant in the "days of
'49" and again, years after, as a prospector in the silver
mines of Nevada. With this introduction we shall let the
Indian poet tell the story of the Humboldt desert:—

Who journeys o'er the desert now,
   Where sinks engulfed the Humboldt river,
Arrested in its sudden flow,
   But pouring in that depth forever.

As if the famished earth would drink
   Adry the tributes of the mountains,
Yet wither on the water's brink,
   And thirst for still unnumbered fountains.

Who journeys o'er that desert now
   Shall see strange sights, I ween, and ghastly;
For he shall trace, awearied, slow,
   Across this waste extended vastly.

The steps of pilgrims westward bound,
   Bound westward to the Land Pacific,
Where hoped-for rest and peace are found,
   And plenty waves her wand prolific.

     *   *   *   *   *   *   *

No sound is heard—a realm of blight,
   Of weird-like silver and brightness
That maketh but a gloom of light,
   Where glimmer shapes of spectral whiteness!

They are the bones that bleaching lie
   Where fell the wearied beasts o'er-driven,

And upward cast his dying eye
　　As if in dumb appeal to heaven.

For lenthening miles on miles that lie,
　　These sad memorials, grim and hoary,
And every whitening heap we spy
　　Doth tell some way-worn pilgrim's story.

Hard by each skeleton there stand
　　The wheels it drew, or warped or shrunken,
And in the drifting, yielding sand
　　The yoke or rusted chain has sunken.

Nor marvel we, if yonder peers,
　　From out some scooped-out grave and shallow,
A human head which fleshless leers
　　With look that doth the place unhallow.
　　　*　　*　　*　　*　　*　　*　　*
But pass we these grim, mouldering things,
　　Decay shall claim as Time may order,
For, offspring of the mountain springs,
　　A river rims the desert border;
With margin green and beautiful,
　　And sparkling waters silver-sounding,
And trees with zephyrs musical,
　　And answering birds with songs abounding;
And velvet flowers of thousand scents,
　　And clambering vines with blossoms crested;
'Twas here the pilgrims pitched their tents,
　　And from their toilsome travel rested.
　　　*　　*　　*　　*　　*　　*　　*
Sad pilgrims o'er life's desert, we,
　　Our tedious journey onward ever;
But rest for us there yet shall be,
　　When camped upon the Heavenly River.

THE FIRST BABY IN CAMP.

THE LAST PROCESSION OF THE "ARGONAUTS."

"Boys," said an old Pacific Coast Pioneer to half a dozen men of the "days of '49," as the conversation turned upon the old golden days of California placer mining, "boys, a curious thing happened me last month while I was spending a few days on the other side of the mountains."

Those addressed as "boys" were men in whose faces "the inaudible and noiseless foot of Time" had left its imprint and whose hair had been powdered by the snows of many winters. Though for years residents of the Comstock, the memory of the old days across the mountains was fresh in the minds of all.

"What happened you, Dick; did you go against faro and win?" said one of the "Old Boys."

"Faro had nothing to do with it, Ben. No, this was a more serious matter—a thing of solemn character and grave import. It was a vision."

"A vision!" cried two or three of the old-timers.

"Our brother is a prophet," said old Ben, "he has visions."

"Neither a prophet nor the son of a prophet," said the old man, "yet what I saw had in it something prophetic. I will relate what occurred and you may judge for yourselves."

"The vision! The vision! Let us have the vision!" cried all present.

"Well, here you have it," said the venerable Argonaut:

"I went one day, while on the California side of the Sierras, to pay a visit to my old mining camp in the mountains. While I was still on the trail leading up from the foothills to the great canyon in which I had mined in the old times, and while I was thinking of the old friends and companions of those days, there came before my eyes a sort of mist and I halted and seated myself on a moss-grown rock. At first it seemed a mere dimness of my eyes, but as I looked about, it appeared that a sort of haze had settled down upon the face of the earth. ' At first I could but dimly see through this mist the trunks of the nearest trees, and large rocks at a little distance looked as unsubstantial as clouds. But as I gazed, the haze took on a golden hue and became thinner and thinner till at last it was quite transparent. Raising my eyes, I saw many persons coming Indian file along a trail that seemed well-beaten and led down the slope of a great mountain. This I suppose to be a part of the Sierra Nevada range. I could see far in the distance snowy peaks that stood sharp and glittering against a deep-blue sky. Below these peaks were dark belts that I know must be forests of pine, while nearer were rounded hills, rutted and red. Those descending the mountain trail formed a long, straggling procession. Seldom were two seen together. Alone and with earnest and thoughtful faces they walked the winding path. All were well advanced in years, and the gait of many was feeble and slow. But slow as were their steps, the advance of the feeble ones was uniform with that of the others. The ground seemed to glide beneath their feet and bear them on. As far as my eyes could reach along up the meandering trail in the direction of the dark pines and snowy peaks, the procession extended—away, away till those composing it dwindled to mere figures and shadows. What could be the meaning of this strange pilgrimage of old men from the mountains down toward the sea? It was an exodus solemn and awful. Who were these sedate venerables and whither were they plodding? As they silently passed along the path at the foot of the jutting rock on which I had found a seat, I rose and gazed upon their fixed and serious countenances in silent awe. The very marrow in my bones seemed to be congealing. It was as though these white-faced old men had brought down with them the chilling atmosphere of the snowy peaks whence they came. At first, all the faces I saw were un-

known to me, yet had a strangely familiar look. It occured
to me that if I had not seen them before I had known their
brothers and all their kinsmen. As I thus stood and wondering gazed, I saw approaching a pilgrim that I knew. I
had lived with him in the same cabin in the olden times;
had loved him as a brother and honored him as a man.
Though I called him by name, he now passed me without
turning his head. No change was seen in his countenance,
and he seemed not to have heard my voice. His features
were fixed and his gaze was forward. While I thus stood
near the trail, still others appeared that I well knew. All
were old-time miners. On, on, along the beaten trail they
tramped. One came who had once long been my partner
in the mountains. Far up in the high Sierras, beside banks
of everlasting snow, we had watched by the same camp-fire
and slept under the same blankets. Him, with confidence,
I called by name, feeling sure that he would halt and tell
me whither this great procession of venerable Argonauts
was journeying—would tell me the meaning of this great
migration toward the broad ocean and the setting sun. But
he, too, passed on in silence and with no change of expres-
sion that told of my voice having reached his ears. On he
moved and new and strange faces appeared and passed.
Women, too, occasionally passed along, some alone and some
moving side by side with aged men. The locks of the
women were white and their faces showed the foot-prints
of Time. All were women of the old days. 'Can it be possible,' said I to myself, 'that some new and golden region
has been discovered, the fame of which has put in motion
all these gold diggers of the olden days?' As I thus solilo-
quized, I became aware that I had imperceptibly moved
downward in the direction in which the procession was
winding along, although I had not taken a step. It was as
if the ground on which I stood had gently glided down-

ward and forward; already the snowy peaks of the mountains seemed mere piles of clouds against the sky and the
belt of pines had faded from sight. Turning and looking
in the direction in which the gaze of all in the procession
seemed fixed, I found myself standing beside a great precipice. At the brink of this vast gulf, the, trail along which
moved the silent train, abruptly ended. All below was
black as night, and darkness as a vapor rolled up against
the precipice, often surging over and hiding its brink.
Thus it happened that not a few pilgrims, unaware of what
was before them, without change of gait or alteration of
mien, strode forward and were suddenly engulfed in the
billows of darkness, their forms dissolving and mingling with
the mist. Others apparently saw at the last moment where
another step would carry them and drew back in alarm as
they felt the chill of the black mist, but soon composing
their features to their former placidity, they boldly moved
on and in an instant had taken the plunge into the dark,
unfathomable abyss. Such as were still moving forward
along the path seemed neither to observe nor heed the sudden dropping off of those who had but a moment before
been walking in advance; composedly as ever they continued on their way until they in turn disappeared from sight.
Looking back toward the now dimly discernable mountains,
I saw that some in the ranks of the pilgrims occasionally
made little excursions from the path, but always returned
to it in a short time, though at a lower point. All their
steps, move as they might, ever tended downward to the
point of final departure into the gloom. I noticed that
some in the procession, and often very aged men, carried
on their backs bundles of blankets, or had with them
mining tools, which did not fall from their hands until they
took their last step and became of the mist. Shading my
eyes with my hands, I gazed long and searchingly toward

the point, far away, on which the eyes of all in the procession seemed fixed when they took the fatal plunge. Looking steadily out over a vast expanse, which seemed a sea— yet more a sea of air and silvery haze than of water—I was able presently to make out, dimly and at a great distance, a wide golden shore that seemed to lift and shimmer as do objects seen in a mirage. In the waving and quivering light that hung over this far-away shore, I caught glimpses of domes and spires as of a mighty city, with a glittering world that stretched beyond all till lost to sight in a purple mist. Dropping my eyes again upon the sea, I could dimly make out bright forms passing to and fro beyond the dark vapors that surged and beat along the great precipice. Turning again toward the trail that wound away up the face of the great mountain, I saw coming down toward the precipice a figure that startled me. It appeared strangely familiar. I said to myself: 'Here marches down another grizzled Argonaut to take the fatal plunge. Great was my awe, as the pilgrim came up, to see in him myself. It was just as if I had been standing before a mirror. Even as I gazed, I saw myself moving step by step down toward the brink of the precipice and the dark rolling gulf. I dropped upon the ground and clutched at a rock, shrieking in agony: 'My God! I shall soon go over!' With this cry, the golden mists about me cleared away; the mountains took their natural form, and I saw winding lonely and rugged before me the unused trail that led up the canyon to my old camp of the days of '49. I found myself reclining against and clutching the rock on which I had taken a seat when the yellow haze first settled down about me. For a time I could hardly believe I was still safe and my heart beat so violently that for some moments I could only breath in gasps. Now don't tell me that I fell asleep on that rock and was dreaming. I was as wide awake as I am at this moment; it was a vision—a vision such as poor mortals are sometimes permitted to see."

STAGE ROBBERIES.

Before the days of railroads, stage robberies were of very frequent occurrence, both in California and Nevada. Then the stages carried large amounts of treasure in gold and silver, and the "road agents" often made great "hauls." The stages running over the Sierras between California and Nevada were often halted and plundered. About the first thing the highwayman called for after halting a coach, was Wells,Fargo and Co.'s treasure box. "Hand down that box!" was an order that many a driver was very unwillingly obliged to obey in those old days. The passengers were generally made to alight, when they were ranged in a row on the roadside under guard of a shot gun, to be presently searched and stripped of their coin and valuables. Many were the robberies of this kind that took place on the various roads leading out of Virginia City, Nevada, before railroad connection was made with that place. Sometimes the treasure box was blown open and plundered on the spot, but it was more frequently carried off that its contents might be examined at leisure. We have not space in which to give particulars in regard to the many stage robberies that occurred in the early days, therefore select one that is a fair sample of all, all being much alike in their leading features.

On Thursday night, June 11, 1868, about 12 o'clock, the overland stage was stopped and robbed in Six-mile canyon at a point about five miles east of Virginia City, Nevada. The robbers were three in number, were armed with double-barreled shot-guns, and were completely masked by white cloths tied over their faces. There were six passengers aboard, four gentlemen and two ladies. All these were plundered of their money and such other valuables as the robbers discovered.

The robbery occurred just below the Sugar-loaf mountain, near a bridge across the canyon, in Flowery mining district. The robbers were lying in wait for the stage, and the' first the passengers knew of the matter was when the team which was moving at a slow pace, came to a halt and the barrel of a shot gun was thrust in at each of the doors of the coach. One of the robbers stood at the heads of the lead horses with his gun leveled on the driver, who was ordered down from his seat. The driver was "Baldy" Green, whose record as a victim of "hold-ups" has already been referred to in these pages.

"Get out, you folks inside!" said one of the robbers as he thrust the muzzle of his gun into the coach.

"What is the matter?" innocently inquired a passenger who had not noticed the gun.

"Get out! Get out of there, I tell you, and damned quick, or you'll find out what's the matter in a way you won't like!" cried the robber.

The barrels of the two shot guns glittering in the light of the stage lamps were powerful persuaders and all made haste to obey the robber's order. As soon as the passengers were out and ranged in line, the man who did the talking, and who appeared to be the leader of the gang, hastily searched the men for arms and then more at leisure "went through" the whole party for money and valuables.

Most of the passengers were old residents of the Pacific Coast and were sufficiently well informed in regard to the etiquette of such occasions to be able to conduct themselves with a degree of propriety satisfactory to the road agents. All in the coach perfectly comprehended the situation the moment they saw the barrels of the guns and having litle fear of their lives were able to give all their thoughts to the preservation of their property. The passengers aboard were David B. McGee and his wife, of one of the valley towns of California; Antoine Aguago, also of Califor-

nia; Miss Susan Hodgen, of the Comstock; Barney Dougherty, an empleye of the stage company; and Dr. C. W. Heath,
then a practicing physician of Virginia City, now dead.　Of
Mr. McGee the robbers took $8. in coin and a common sil-
ver watch, but not liking the looks of the watch, they returned it.　From Dr. Heath they took $300. and a gold
watch worth $300.; of Antoine Aguago, $325. and a fine
chronometer valued at $250.; while "Baldy" Green was re-
lieved of about $10.　Of the ladies they got nothing.　Mrs.
McGee had $900. concealed in the bosom of her dress, but
she was only superficially searched and the money was not
discovered.　Miss Hogden had a gold watch and some
money but was not searched.　Barney Dougherty, a hostler
who had for some time been employed on the stage route,
had $200. in gold in a buckskin purse which he cunningly
managed to slip down the back of his neck while clumsily
getting out of the coach.　The purse was not discovered by
the robbers, who, finding six bits in silver in his pockets,
took him for a poor, impecunious fellow and passed him by
without much ceremony.　Dr. Heath tried to slip his watch,
which he greatly prized, into his boot, but was detected in
the act and the watch confiscated, smuggling not being tol-
erated.　Antoine Aguago had in a pocket book a check for
$3,000 and managed, before getting out of the coach, to
slip the book under a cushion where it was overlooked by
the robbers.　When they had secured the money and valuables of the passengers, the "road agents" threw the
mails and baggage out upon the ground, and, retaining
three bags of bullion, two of them drove the coach up the
canyon.　The mails and baggage were not rifled.　The
third robber, who seemed leader of the gang, now ordered
all the passengers to take up their march to a ravine in the
vicinity, telling the driver to pick up his whip and carry it
with him.　On arriving at the ravine the passengers were

formed in line and told to keep a few feet apart. This was to prevent them from talking and plotting together without being overheard. When all were in line they were ordered to march up the revine, the "boss" robber walking behind with his shotgun ready to preserve order in the ranks. In this order they were marched up the ravine a distance of over half a mile, when they were halted and seated together in a row. The robber kept guard over them with his gun in an alert and able-bodied manner until after 1 o'clock in the morning. He was a man of stalwart form and his prisoners guessed his weight to be about 165 pounds. A solid man to tackle, yet Aguago, who was a powerful man, was for attacking him. He was in favor of making a rush on the guard who at times stood silently before his prisoners, then at times patroled before them. It was the plan of Aguago to rush upon the robber with rocks as he turned in his promedade, knock him down and take possession of his gun. He whispered his plan to Mr. McGee, who sat next to him, but that gentleman refused, on account of the presence of his wife, to take any desperate chances. Finally the robber took out his watch, looked at the time and then told his prisoners that they should all remain quietly seated as they were for twenty-five minutes, when he would come for them with the coach. He impressed it upon them that they were on no account to move until he came for them, and told them that if any of them came down to the mouth of the ravine they would find some of his men ready to attend to their cases. He then marched off. After waiting half an hour the passengers started down the ravine to the road. When the road was reached, Mr. McGee went to the Lady Bryan mill, procured a horse and hastening up the canyon to Virginia City gave the alarm, the remainder of the passengers following on foot. About two miles up the canyon from where the stage was stopped, coach and team were found—the horses being tied to some bushes by the roadside. At this point the two robbers who drove off with the coach had finished their part of the work by breaking open the treasure box and robbing it of its contents. They got but $169, four small packages of coin, and overlooked several packages that were in the express pocket book. The three bars of silver bullion were worth $3,584.06. Mr. Latham, of Wells, Fargo & Co.'s express, with several others, went to the scene of the robbery in the morning about daylight, and after a long search succeeded in finding two of the stolen bars in the sage-brush only a short distance from the road. The third bar was not found.

This robbery, and several others it was afterwards discovered, was the work of the Jack Davis gang, of Flowery district. They were arrested for this robbery, but it could not be brought home to them. Long afterwards they were arrested for a stage robbery on the Geiger Grade, convicted and sent to the State prison. A fine gold watch taken from Judge Richard Rising at the time of the Geiger Grade robbery, and found in Jack Davis' cabin, cunningly concealed in the ornamental mouldings of a desk, fastened that affair upon Jack. Soon the whole business was given away, when it was found that Jack and his partners had leased a quartz mill and pretended to be working the ore of a mine, their usual business being to work up into saleable shape the silver bars captured in their night raids on the stages.

FASTEST PONY EXPRESS TIME.

The best time made between Reno and Virginia with ponies and riders was 61 minutes for the Pacific Express and 58 minutes for Wells, Fargo & Co. Ten changes of ponies was made between the two points. This was in 1869 on an occasion when a job had been put up by J. W. Hemenway, the well-known blacksmith, and several other sportive gentlemen to have the Pacific pony beat Wells, Fargo & Co. The conspiritors had quietly got all the fastest nags they could find in that part of the State and shipped them into the line of the Pacific Express ponies. When this was accomplished, they were willing to bet five to one on their favorite coming in ahead. They took all the bets they could get, putting up every cent they had or could raise on the proposition. This little game had leaked out and prompt measures were taken to checkmate it. W. P. Bennett, the efficient superintending manager of Wells, Fargo & Co.'s horse department, was equal to the occasion and prepared for their fast nags. Mr. Latham, the chief agent of Wells, Fargo & Co.'s Virginia office had said "Mr. Bennett, I've got $500 bet on this race and I want you to beat those fellows."

All right," confidently responded Mr. Bennett. "They've got to make it in 58 minutes or I'll beat 'em," and beat them he did. The fast nags wrung into the Pacific line by the Hemenway crowd were swift enough on good ground, but not particularly experienced in up-hill traveling. Bennett went among the stage teams and picked out some of the best and fastest horses, putting them on the road as ponies. Commencing at the foot of the Geiger Grade, he strung these long-winded stage horses all the way up and across the mountain road to Virginia City—they were what carried the day. The Pacific fast nags weakened when urged up the steep grade, but the lively old stage horses galloped right along up without any trouble. On the occasion of the race, the most noted of many, Bennett, himself, rode from Steamboat creek to the Six-Mile House at the Summit of the Geiger Grade, and Archie Morris rode into Wells, Fargo & Co.'s office at Virginia. George Gray took the first heat out of Reno, there being four riders in the entire distance. Previous to this famous race, there had been much heavy betting on the ponies, all the sports becoming interested; but this ended it, so far as they were concerned.

About four weeks later, in '69, there was a great race between the stages of the rival companies. In this race Billy Hodges drove for Wells, Fargo & Co. and Charley Carroll for the Pacific Express Co. Hodges drove six horses and Carroll drove four. Carroll got the lead at Reno and kept it as far as Huffaker's Station. Hodge then got in ahead and kept the foot of the Geiger Grade when Carroll cut in ahead and kept ahead till he reached the Ophir House, on the Grade. There Hodge got in ahead again, and from there the coaches kept close together. When they struck the north end of C Street, there was room enough. Carroll pulled up alongside of Hodge, but found it impossible to pass him, so evenly were the two teams matched as regards speed and strength. The two stages drove into the city side by side amid the shouts and cheers of thousands of excited spectators who thronged the sidewalks, filled the balconies and covered the housetops. Time, 1:32. Distance, 22 miles.

Colonel Avery, the well-known mining and mill superintendent, was at Reno, where the stages started on the aforesaid race. He had a fine light buggy and a pair of horses that he thought the finest and best on the Comstock. The Colonel rashly remarked that he would beat the two racing stages into Virginia or kill his horses. He followed the stages till near the White House, half way up the grade, when his horses were so fatigued as to be ready to drop, stopping and refusing to move. The Colonel very sensibly came to the conclusion that if he urged his good animals further as he had done, then death would be the result, therefore gave them the much needed rest, and traveled the remainder of the distance at a leisurely style of gait, getting through an hour and a half behind the stage.